50 PRAYERS

for Our NATION

Missionary Julian Marie Walker

*Book One The Lord hear Our Prayers
Amen*

Completed with love

All rights reserved.
Copyright © Julian Marie Walker

No part of this publication may be reproduced or transmitted in any form or by any means without the written permission of the publisher.
ISBN: 978-1-956884-27-2

Contributing Editor: All services completed by Imprint Productions, Inc.

Cover Design: All services completed by Imprint Productions, Inc.

Printed in the United States of America Published by Imprint Productions, Inc.

First Edition 2024

Table Of Contents

PART 1

1] The Covenant Keeping God

Dear Father God, You have shown us the signs that You are the Divine and Supreme God almighty who holds all the true power.

Today I look through my window, and my eyes behold the beauty and the promise You made us many generations ago.

Father, it was the sign of the Rainbow and its shine through the gray skies and rain.

It was red, yellow, and mixtures of blue and green.

I could not help but think, You were reminding Your people that You are The Great I am.

Accordingly, You will keep The Promise.

As Your word states in **Gen 9: 13 I set My rainbow in the cloud, and it Shall be for a sign of my covenant between Me and the earth.**

Glory to God, I repeat Glory to God in highest.

Thank You, God, for who You are in Heaven and Earth.

Amen and Amen
Missionary Julian Marie Walker

Dear reader!

Today, we take our faith to a higher level in Jesus Christ, regarding Your family, health, and finances. Therefore, for every good and pure thing You believe in God for, You can join the Spiritual Agreement page. Write down Your request and sign it!

____

____

Sign____

We the body of believers ask God for supernatural miracles and manifestations according to his word John 14:14, " If ye shall ask anything in my name, I will do it". Thank You, Lord Jesus, in advance for Your care and abundant good blessing in the Mighty name of Jesus!

Amen.

Sincerely, Julian Marie Walker
Author/ Intercessor/ Missionary

2] Prayer to the Holy Father…

Father God, Great are You, Lord.
I thank You for this new day.

Amen
Missionary Julian Marie Walker

Dear reader!

Today, we take our faith to a higher level in Jesus Christ, regarding Your family, health, and finances. Therefore, for every good and pure thing You believe in God for, You can join the Spiritual Agreement page. Write down Your request and sign it!

____

____

Sign____

We the body of believers ask God for supernatural miracles and manifestations according to his word John 14:14, " If ye shall ask anything in my name, I will do it". Thank You, Lord Jesus, in advance for Your care and abundant good blessing in the Mighty name of Jesus!

Amen.

Sincerely, Julian Marie Walker
Author/ Intercessor/ Missionary

3] The Prayer for the Righteousness of God to take over.

Father God, we come before Your presence with expectations that when we asked You. So today, I ask You for health and strength that You who began a good work in me will do it for me till the day of Jesus Christ our Lord.

Father, it's in my weakness that Your powers work so great and beautiful. So, I give You thanks and Praise for the things You are still able to do through me.

Father forgive them for they know not what they have done. I am human and I also put my faith and trust in You. My wonder-working God today, tomorrow, and yesterday I pray for me, my children and my grandchildren calling out their names one by one to be blessed to the point of being blessed with the fruit of Your Spirits of God. I pray for my home, my finances, and all that You are given to be blessed abundantly. I pray for wisdom, guidance and protection and any host that dares to come near my family falls back in the pit of hell.

I pray for my neighbors and neighborhood that we will be men and women of God and be wealthy and rich spiritually, emotionally, and financially. Lord, I pray for my City and States and Country. Lord, I pray for the family and good friends wherever they may be. I pray for World Peace around the country and the World. I pray for all those who lead, let them lead with integrity and ethical principles and all those who follow do likewise.

Father God this prayer I bring to You with uttermost urgency. Father God whatever their name, their position or job title let today be the last day that they operate without You oh God.

I call upon You Lord God to see that every system works and functions on purpose; it was created and if it is broken then fix it. According to **Philippians 2:13 "for it is God who works in You to will and to act to fulfill his good purpose."** Lord, according to Your desire, God meet us where we need You the most. I pray for grace and mercy to take charge and give Your people freedom and peace.

Lord, I thank You in advance for all You are about to do. In Jesus' everlasting name, I pray…
Let it be done. Thank You!

Amen and Amen
Missionary Julian Marie Walker

Dear reader!

Today, we take our faith to a higher level in Jesus Christ, regarding Your family, health, and finances. Therefore, for every good and pure thing You believe in God for, You can join the Spiritual Agreement page. Write down Your request and sign it!

____

____

Sign____

We the body of believers ask God for supernatural miracles and manifestations according to his word John 14:14, " If ye shall ask anything in my name, I will do it". Thank You, Lord Jesus, in advance for Your care and abundant good blessing in the Mighty name of Jesus!

Amen.

Sincerely, Julian Marie Walker
Author/ Intercessor/ Missionary

4] Prayer Of Giving Thanks in the 12-hour

The prayer of thanks has great power to prevail.
Father God, we show up and show out at twelve hours through the gift of the Holy Spirit. As the twelve disciples did for You at Your request. Father, we thank You for all things good and pleasing to Your sight. May we sing hallelujah and dance in Your presence.

We thank You for Your saving grace according to Your promise. We thank You for being the God who gave Salvation. We are thankful for peace and harmony.

We thank You for Your guidance.

We thank You for being a Psalm 91 God that shelters Your people in secret the Most High.

We thank You for being as bright as Morning Star.

We thank You for being The Lord of our Salvation God.

We thank God for being Our Psalm 23 God.

We thank You For Being our Psalm 100 God.

We thank You for being our everlasting God.

We thank You for being a friend at times God.

We thank You for Your Holy Spirit God.

We thank You for the land flowing with milk and honey.

We thank You for drawing closer to us than a brother.

We thank You for health and strength.

We thank You for healing our minds and bodies.

We thank You for Your focus, wisdom, and knowledge.

We thank You all that all is righteous in Your sight.

We thank You for Your teaching.

We thank You for Your advice.

We as a whole body thank You for the hem of the garment.

We thank You for ministering to us daily.

We thank You for making all things new again.

We thank You for the people You have saved including me.

We thank You for Your compassion.

We thank You for Your integrity.

We thank You for love, peace, and happiness.

We are thankful that what is impossible for man, is not impossible for You.

We thank You for setting a global example of kindness.

We thank You for giving us hope in You.

We thank our childlike faith for believing in the impossible.

We thank You for allowing us to use Your powerful name.

We thank You for Your nature, name, and powers.

We thank You for opening new and good doors.

We thank You for closing the bad doors.

We are thankful for traveling mercies.

We thank You for Divine favors.

We thank You for the promises of God.

We thank You for actively answering prayers.

We thank You for Your freedom.

We thank You for Your Hallelujah and Amen.

We thank You forevermore in Jesus' name.

Amen and Amen
Missionary Julian Marie Walker

Dear reader!

Today, we take our faith to a higher level in Jesus Christ, regarding Your family, health, and finances. Therefore, for every good and pure thing You believe in God for, You can join the Spiritual Agreement page. Write down Your request and sign it!

____

____

Sign____

We the body of believers ask God for supernatural miracles and manifestations according to his word John 14:14, " If ye shall ask anything in my name, I will do it". Thank You, Lord Jesus, in advance for Your care and abundant good blessing in the Mighty name of Jesus!

Amen.

Sincerely, Julian Marie Walker
Author/ Intercessor/ Missionary

5] The prayer of Restoration has great power to prevail for God's People.

Abba Father and Divine Covenant keeping God, I appeal for financial restoration. I pray that all that has been stolen and should be returned with lifetime interest to protect the integrity of Your Kingdom. I pray for Your divine healing, guidance, and protection.

Father, You promised that nothing or none can stop the blessing provided for us. Father, You said that all we have to do is ask anything in Your name Jesus Christ and it will be done according to You. Father, You said we should seek, and we shall find according to Your will. Father, You said knock and the door will be open according to Your plans.

Therefore, in agreement with Your word and in the name of the Father, Son, and the Holy Spirit, I thank You in advance for what You are doing now in this lifetime.
Amen and Amen

Missionary Julian Marie Walker

Dear reader!

Today, we take our faith to a higher level in Jesus Christ, regarding Your family, health, and finances. Therefore, for every good and pure thing You believe in God for, You can join the Spiritual Agreement page. Write down Your request and sign it!

____

____

Sign____

We the body of believers ask God for supernatural miracles and manifestations according to his word John 14:14, " If ye shall ask anything in my name, I will do it". Thank You, Lord Jesus, in advance for Your care and abundant good blessing in the Mighty name of Jesus!

Amen.

Sincerely, Julian Marie Walker
Author/ Intercessor/ Missionary

6] Praying with Purpose…   There will be Victory in Jesus

In his name God Almighty, I pray.

In the plans of God concerning me. In my Prayers.

In every area of my life.

In my home and my houses.

In my children's lives.

My purpose.

In my vision.

In my Goals.

In my health.

My love.

My finance.

Most importantly for the seed that I have planted for the purpose of God's Glory.

Selah

Missionary Julian Marie Walker

Dear reader!

Today, we take our faith to a higher level in Jesus Christ, regarding Your family, health, and finances. Therefore, for every good and pure thing You believe in God for, You can join the Spiritual Agreement page. Write down Your request and sign it!

____

____

Sign____

We the body of believers ask God for supernatural miracles and manifestations according to his word John 14:14, " If ye shall ask anything in my name, I will do it". Thank You, Lord Jesus, in advance for Your care and abundant good blessing in the Mighty name of Jesus!

Amen.

Sincerely, Julian Marie Walker
Author/ Intercessor/ Missionary

7] **Prayer for New Blessings and more**

Most Gracious Father, I give thanks unto You this day. Your word states that everything that has breath gives praise and thanksgiving onto the LORD.

Psalm 150.6 Let everything that has breath praise ye the Lord. Oh, Abba father, we humble Yourself to You who is Lord of all Lords, Therefore may Your Power increase in the word You spoke many months ago.

I thank You for Your wisdom, knowledge and understanding in all areas of my life.

In Jesus name I pray.

Amen.

Missionary Julian Marie Walker

Dear reader!

Today, we take our faith to a higher level in Jesus Christ, regarding Your family, health, and finances. Therefore, for every good and pure thing You believe in God for, You can join the Spiritual Agreement page. Write down Your request and sign it!

____

____

Sign____

We the body of believers ask God for supernatural miracles and manifestations according to his word John 14:14, " If ye shall ask anything in my name, I will do it". Thank You, Lord Jesus, in advance for Your care and abundant good blessing in the Mighty name of Jesus!

Amen.

Sincerely, Julian Marie Walker
Author/ Intercessor/ Missionary

8] God is Worthy, Praise Him

Heavenly Father, Thank You for this day.

Father God, we come before Your presence giving honor, praise, and worship unto You our great King. Father You Lord are great, **For the Lord is great, and greatly to be praised: he is to be feared above all gods. Psalm 96:4.**

Thank You for giving us the opportunity to always keep us in Your love and care. Father God, I thank You for healing, grace, and mercy.

Father God, I thank You for the miracles that the world doesn't see, You didn't have to do them, but You did it anyway.

Father this morning, I thank You for more life and abundant blessing. So, Father all this has been said You already know therefore, I pray for my children and grandchildren. I pray for my home, my family and friends, and their friends. I pray for my neighborhood, my city, State, and my Country.

I pray for my nation and all the people to be healed and come to know You, Father God, as their Lord and savior. We give thanks in advance for those who will come to know You as personally as I know You. Father God the air is light and clean this morning.

Therefore, Father, I am trusting that my prayer will get to You and be granted for Your people by way of the Holy Spirit.

This morning, I called on my way making a covenant keeping God. Therefore, Your words declare Lord, **If we live in the Spirit, let us also walk in the Spirit. Galatian 5:25**

I am asking You to help all those in need during this natural disaster. Help and give them peace as they come to know what mighty God You are and that You will never forsake them.

That being said, bless all those who help them. May You replenish their shelf and store houses. Father, may You send a good and honest man of God to restore their lives. In the name of Jesus, we bind up the scammer and the thieves planning to take disadvantage of Your people. Father, I pray for Churches and schools this morning in the name of Jesus.

I pray for all government and parliamentary systems this morning. May they be managed by honest people with integrity.

I pray for all people working for Your people, minister, teachers, nurses, doctor, lawyer, clerk, storekeeper, firemen, policeman, soldiers, daycare providers, everyone and whoever works to empower Your peoples.

Father I was one told that serving is an act of God. Father, I just ask for their professionalism and empathy to manifest to Your people. Good people bring advancement to the Kingdom and Your people. I am thankful for wisdom, strength and overflowing with the Holy Spirit's love and grace. Thank You for always showing up and showing out when I need You the most. Thank You for always providing hope and favor....

In Jesus name.
Amen
Missionary Julian Marie Walker

Dear reader!

Today, we take our faith to a higher level in Jesus Christ, regarding Your family, health, and finances. Therefore, for every good and pure thing You believe in God for, You can join the Spiritual Agreement page. Write down Your request and sign it!

____

____

Sign____

We the body of believers ask God for supernatural miracles and manifestations according to his word John 14:14, " If ye shall ask anything in my name, I will do it". Thank You, Lord Jesus, in advance for Your care and abundant good blessing in the Mighty name of Jesus!

Amen.

Sincerely, Julian Marie Walker
Author/ Intercessor/ Missionary

9] Powerful Hallelujah Prayers for God's People

Heavenly Father, I thank You for this day, which is so precious.

Thank You for newfound wisdom and revelation. Father, thank You for meeting me where I am this morning, emotional, in my mind and body. Thank You for covering me through the night. This morning with honor to You first and foremost. Thank You for ministering to me all through the Holy Spirit.

Father, You hold me and guide me in every circumstance. Lord, I thank You for strength, faith, hope and love. Abba this morning I pray for Your creation starting with man, woman, boys, and girls. That they will love one another and care for each as You do for them. Father, we pray this morning for divine harmony and peace. Peace be still in the name of the Lord Jesus Christ.

Father this morning I pray that You Father God go to work on behalf of You people and make every plan of the enemy be put to shame and never to cause You hurt again. Father binds up all wounds as the greatest physician and doctor I know is Jehovah Rapha. Help Your children's father that they mind work according to Your plan, what good great God You are to us.

Father this morning, Spirit of living God we cry out to You to dislike and cause the evil plans of the enemy to fail. Yes, Father I mean fail. Father it time stop them dead in the track so they can never hurt or cause Your people to fall again. Father, I know, and I trust that You can do all things. Bring Your children freshwater to do Your will. Hallelujah in name of the Lord. Father it's a new day, let old things pass away and the new to come now in the name of Jesus.

Lord Your People tarry no more because of You will for them to prosper in Jesus name. Father, we give You the Jehovah Japha who provides all thanks, so we give thanks in advance. Thus, You are Jehovah Shalom who give peace to Your people. Father You are the Alpha and Omega I trust that Your will be done on earth as it is heaven. Father we Your people are mindful to give You and only all the praise and honor.

We pray for children and Families and in Jesus name. Father it would be me if I did pray for my home, neighborhood, City, my County, my State, my Country, my adjoining cities and state and the Nations. Father, I pray for the Judicial system, Congress system and legislative system, House of Parliament and Representative. We pray for unity and advancement for all Your people. Father was for the School, College, and Universities.

We pray for the churches, Court system, Welfare system, Defense system. Police system, firefighter departments, transportation system include airline system, Military, Economy system especially the banking system. Entertainment system and Media system, Healthcare system, taxes and Insurance system, Agriculture system, Big pharma manufacturer companies, every government system, and every industry that services Your people needs.

We Pray for good men and women of God to rise up and lead with integrity starting this day. We pray for wisdom for all who lead and all those who follow. **The prayer of a righteous man has great power to prevail.**

I thank the Lord for grace and favor in Jesus' name. I pray.

Hallelujah and Amen

Dear reader!

Today, we take our faith to a higher level in Jesus Christ, regarding Your family, health, and finances. Therefore, for every good and pure thing You believe in God for, You can join the Spiritual Agreement page. Write down Your request and sign it!

____

____

Sign____

We the body of believers ask God for supernatural miracles and manifestations according to his word John 14:14, " If ye shall ask anything in my name, I will do it". Thank You, Lord Jesus, in advance for Your care and abundant good blessing in the Mighty name of Jesus!

Amen.

Sincerely, Julian Marie Walker
Author/ Intercessor/ Missionary

10] Night Prayers for Helping People

Father God, we thank You that the Sun rises, and the moon comes out tonight through the gray skies. Thank You for our daily Bread and so much more. I pray You send help for Your people according to their need in Jesus name.

Amen
Missionary Julian Marie Walker

Dear reader!

Today, we take our faith to a higher level in Jesus Christ, regarding Your family, health, and finances. Therefore, for every good and pure thing You believe in God for, You can join the Spiritual Agreement page. Write down Your request and sign it!

____

____

Sign____

We the body of believers ask God for supernatural miracles and manifestations according to his word John 14:14, " If ye shall ask anything in my name, I will do it". Thank You, Lord Jesus, in advance for Your care and abundant good blessing in the Mighty name of Jesus!

Amen.

Sincerely, Julian Marie Walker
Author/ Intercessor/ Missionary

PART 2

11] Morning Prayer - 6:00am

Prayers of Intercede The prayer of a righteous man has great power to prevail.

Abba Father here I come, giving You thanks and praise for keeping me through the night. This morning, I pray for all Your people because if they matter to You then they matter to me. Father this morning I ask You to touch all those that are in charge that govern and rule over our Cities, Counties, States and Country. Father, I pray that they put Your people's needs first and do what is right for all people. **Give them a clean heart and new purpose to serve with compassion, love, fairness, and integrity.**

Father may their moral compass be center enclosure for all people regardless of race, origin, or sex. Father when You died on the cross, You died for all mankind to be redeemed and ransom for the edification to honor and praise You. Therefore, when we accept You as our Lord and savior, we are saved. Holy Father according to Your word You have the power to intercede.

I pray and believe that You God can change hearts one by one.

Father Your word states, **And he who searches our hearts knows the mind of the Spirit, because the Spirit intercedes for God's people in accordance with the will of God Romans 8:27** .Therefore with my faith I am giving You many thanks and praise for Your divine intervention. Thank You again Lord, as angels are at work right now in the mighty name of Jesus. Thank You for this heart-to-heart blessing.

So be it and Amen.

Missionary Julian Marie Walker

Dear reader!

Today, we take our faith to a higher level in Jesus Christ, regarding Your family, health, and finances. Therefore, for every good and pure thing You believe in God for, You can join the Spiritual Agreement page. Write down Your request and sign it!

____

____

Sign____

We the body of believers ask God for supernatural miracles and manifestations according to his word John 14:14, " If ye shall ask anything in my name, I will do it". Thank You, Lord Jesus, in advance for Your care and abundant good blessing in the Mighty name of Jesus!

Amen.

Sincerely, Julian Marie Walker
Author/ Intercessor/ Missionary

12] Noon Day Prayer for family

The prayer of a righteous man has great power to prevail.

Our Father, as I recalled, You said come all who are faithful! Not because we are perfect, beautiful, or rich. Even though these qualities and things are wonderful in the sight of mankind. But we choose compassion and wisdom.

Father God, You ask us to keep thy Status. Therefore, we come in the name of the Father God, his son Jesus Christ and Holy Spirit giving thanks first for family, friends, and guardians of the faith, so that we may be triumphant and have the victory over all things concerning our lives. Father, I present to You my petition of hopes through faith, that nothing is impossible for You in Justice.

Amen

Missionary Julian Marie Walker

Dear reader!

Today, we take our faith to a higher level in Jesus Christ, regarding Your family, health, and finances. Therefore, for every good and pure thing You believe in God for, You can join the Spiritual Agreement page. Write down Your request and sign it!

____

____

Sign____

We the body of believers ask God for supernatural miracles and manifestations according to his word John 14:14, " If ye shall ask anything in my name, I will do it". Thank You, Lord Jesus, in advance for Your care and abundant good blessing in the Mighty name of Jesus!

Amen.

Sincerely, Julian Marie Walker
Author/ Intercessor/ Missionary

13] The Prayer asking God for Clean Heart

Heavenly father, I open my heart to You.

Search me and try me and if there is anything that is not of
You remove it.

Father God, please remove any thing that does not work
according to Your plans and purposes

Please don't leave it empty fill me up till I overflow.

Fill me up with strength, love, grace, peace, divine health,
integrity, wisdom, intelligence, value, worthiness, and the
blessing of fruits of the spirits.

Unto…All who ask to receive. James 11:22

In the name of the Father, His son Jesus Christ,
and the Holy Spirit.

Amen
Missionary Julian Marie Walker

Dear reader!

Today, we take our faith to a higher level in Jesus Christ, regarding Your family, health, and finances. Therefore, for every good and pure thing You believe in God for, You can join the Spiritual Agreement page. Write down Your request and sign it!

____

____

Sign____

We the body of believers ask God for supernatural miracles and manifestations according to his word John 14:14, " If ye shall ask anything in my name, I will do it". Thank You, Lord Jesus, in advance for Your care and abundant good blessing in the Mighty name of Jesus!

Amen.

Sincerely, Julian Marie Walker
Author/ Intercessor/ Missionary

14] Prayers We War in the name of Jesus

The spirit moved this morning. This morning, I War
in name of Jesus. We cancel out all demonic plans,
arrangement, plots. The devil has made up with their lie
snake tongue put hook in it Lord. Let the pocket bleed out
for all they have done to poor and innocent people. Father
this is Your promise that when the burden is too heavy to
give to You and You lay it to rest.

So, Father God lay the problem to rest so it can not harm
any other woman or children ever again in life. Way maker God
wake up now, if they running catches them make their fake
signature bleeds, let it run and the paper. Father these people
profess to know You and look what they've done to Your sheep
cause a lot of blood in the lost.

Father come forth and stop them in their tracks and calm
Your Cities. They sold their own people out, father in the name
of Jesus. Accordingly, to the powers invested in me I petition
and plead for Your children. I will not lose faith because all our
hope is in You. Father, they talked about us. They pay people to
bring shame to decent people.

We pray that whoever sees a lie will know it and cast it out.
They plan in their bed at night to pay off people unknown to
buy their soul exchange for partnership. Expose their sinful way
concerning our life, my health, my money, my home, my
children, and my grandchildren. In the name of the Father God,
Father You promised to take care of the sick, children and
widow, in the name Your son Jesus and the holy spirit. Father
brings us to the land that is refreshing for all God's people. Cast
Down those who prey on my family. May today, this day their
last day of victory. Lord, I thank You in advance.

Amen

Dear reader!

Today, we take our faith to a higher level in Jesus Christ, regarding Your family, health, and finances. Therefore, for every good and pure thing You believe in God for, You can join the Spiritual Agreement page. Write down Your request and sign it!

____

____

Sign____

We the body of believers ask God for supernatural miracles and manifestations according to his word John 14:14, " If ye shall ask anything in my name, I will do it". Thank You, Lord Jesus, in advance for Your care and abundant good blessing in the Mighty name of Jesus!

Amen.

Sincerely, Julian Marie Walker
Author/ Intercessor/ Missionary

15] Prayer for Justice Forevermore

My dear Breadring, I greet You in the name of the Father son and the Holy Spirit.If You are holy and honorable, peace be with You. However, if You're not, may my God serve You back for a thousand generations with the fire onto hell that You intend and plotted for me and my children.

I don't write carelessly, so let me lean in with intent. You will pay for all that You are doing and have done to harm me and my children and grandchildren. I am a woman of God, who He has given me the power to declare that You will seek out and [put] to shame. Your tax records will be exposed. The government will seize Your stolen fortune.

May God have mercy on Your sons and daughters.

Father God, You have seen with Your eyes that their heart was corrupt and deceitful, and the money that You intentionally plotted and cheated will never benefit You the wicked another day of Your life. For my name and picture that You have used in Your quest You will die, even though You walk. I did You nothing, but You choose to prey on my family for a few dollars and jealousy. I never want what is Yours, but only what God declares is mine. If You know who I am to God, You will never cross the line.

Well, hear me now in the name of the father the Son and Holy Ghost. You are Done as of this day. This prayer on earth, You should know this prayer stands in the face of the Lord and in his hands forever and ever more. His is the same as my mother's prayers. Money can't buy everything just know, God will forever bless me and my children until thy Kingdom Come.

Just Know, it's So, and Amen and Amen.

Dear reader!

Today, we take our faith to a higher level in Jesus Christ, regarding Your family, health, and finances. Therefore, for every good and pure thing You believe in God for, You can join the Spiritual Agreement page. Write down Your request and sign it!

____

____

Sign____

We the body of believers ask God for supernatural miracles and manifestations according to his word John 14:14, " If ye shall ask anything in my name, I will do it". Thank You, Lord Jesus, in advance for Your care and abundant good blessing in the Mighty name of Jesus!

Amen.

Sincerely, Julian Marie Walker
Author/ Intercessor/ Missionary

16] He is God Almighty.

Father in the name of Jesus Christ gives me strength and courage to pour out from my vessel Your word according to the Gospel of the Living King, my Lord, and Savior Jesus Christ. The Bible states that when You greet them, do so with a kiss, by no way have You come near any of thy people with fleshly thoughts, but with greeting of the Holy Spirit.

Wisdom is given to all those who lack and unto those whom that lives without integrity, unclean heart, hands. See the Bible verse for Yourself. The question is are You so ungodly when You see the miracles and the signs and wonders of God and yet You choose to be in Your flesh. Even when You received the favor of God.

When God love is manifest on earth or the Nation You would not let Your insecurities and conceit self- spread viral lies. I am here to tell You that God who forgives is the first example of forgiveness.

So, I forgive You.

Amen

Dear reader!

Today, we take our faith to a higher level in Jesus Christ, regarding Your family, health, and finances. Therefore, for every good and pure thing You believe in God for, You can join the Spiritual Agreement page. Write down Your request and sign it!

____

____

Sign____

We the body of believers ask God for supernatural miracles and manifestations according to his word John 14:14, " If ye shall ask anything in my name, I will do it". Thank You, Lord Jesus, in advance for Your care and abundant good blessing in the Mighty name of Jesus!

Amen.

Sincerely, Julian Marie Walker
Author/ Intercessor/ Missionary

17] Holy Prayer

Heavenly Father, I rise and lift my hand to You in thanksgiving for a new day. A day of true beauty and splendor living in Your grace and love. Father, I thank You for the miracles You will perform today. Lord, I thank You for giving me a pure heart to pray with You. Father, I continue to pray for my family, all the things that matter to You knowing You can grant all my requests.

I know You provide me, You heal me, You forgive me, You minister to me, You care for me, You protect me, You love me and perfect everything that concerns me. I am confident because the Bible tells me so, You promised that even in the storm of life You will cover me and that my enemy will become my footstool. Acts 2: 34 For David did not ascend to heaven, and yet he said, " 'The Lord said to my Lord: "Sit at my right hand. Acts 2:35 until I make Your enemies a footstool for Your feet." What a mighty God I serve. All my hopes are in You Lord because I have faith and trust in You.

I believed that nothing is impossible for You, and no good things will You withhold from me, and that You Abba Father have given me the grace to see that the people and things You have removed from my life are for my own good. Father, I thank You for revelation and always being in my presence with the powers of the Holy Ghost Spirit. Lord, You said if they were for You, they would continue with You, this I believe.

Thank You for divine favor and making the crooked path straight according to Your plans and purposes. I decree and declare that the devil's plans have failed and are now publicly put to shame for evermore, and cannot come near me, and will never have the Victory in Jesus name. It's with great adoration, I humble myself to the Living God, Jesus Christ my Lord, and Saver. It's in Jesus' Powerful name I pray.

Amen

Dear reader!

Today, we take our faith to a higher level in Jesus Christ, regarding Your family, health, and finances. Therefore, for every good and pure thing You believe in God for, You can join the Spiritual Agreement page. Write down Your request and sign it!

____

____

Sign____

We the body of believers ask God for supernatural miracles and manifestations according to his word John 14:14, " If ye shall ask anything in my name, I will do it". Thank You, Lord Jesus, in advance for Your care and abundant good blessing in the Mighty name of Jesus!

Amen.

Sincerely, Julian Marie Walker
Author/ Intercessor/ Missionary

Our Father Who heart is in heaven hallowed be thy name, thy kingdom come. Give us this day our daily bread and forgive us for our trespasses, as we forgive those who trespass against us. Father leads us not into temptation….But deliver from all evil for thy is Your kingdom. For You God reigns and has the Power and the Glory. Forever and ever more.

According to Your words, Lord it clearly states in Your book of **James 5:16 "Therefore confess Your sins to each other and pray for each other so that You may be healed.** Also, According to the word of Jesus Christ, **"The prayer of a righteous man has great power to prevail."** Father God, You see, and You know of it all so, it is with a clean and upright heart I pray for You in the name of Jesus.

Grateful is thy faithfulness.

Amen

Dear reader!

Today, we take our faith to a higher level in Jesus Christ, regarding Your family, health, and finances. Therefore, for every good and pure thing You believe in God for, You can join the Spiritual Agreement page. Write down Your request and sign it!

____

____

Sign____

We the body of believers ask God for supernatural miracles and manifestations according to his word John 14:14, " If ye shall ask anything in my name, I will do it". Thank You, Lord Jesus, in advance for Your care and abundant good blessing in the Mighty name of Jesus!

Amen.

Sincerely, Julian Marie Walker
Author/ Intercessor/ Missionary

19] Prayer to Extinguishing People's Evil Acts

Most Gracious Father I come in name of Father Lord Jesus, Your son, and the Holy Spirit. To declare that this day is a new beginning, the enemy and imposter that we see this day will be locked up and bound up forever never to hurt or cause harm to Your people again.

Father God, they have plotted and planned, steal, and lie using Your name for too long. I declare that they let loose the children's wealth and if they did let it go, then give them back their medicine, now they will be robbed back from them today. They will be leveled by the IRS and charge back for PP loan if the stolen property is stolen.

They will experience a government seizure in savings until they do good. They have pretended to be fair minded human beings for too long, but they are not fit to be called Holy people. They are wolves in sheep's clothing.

Lord God, anyone that has to put Your people down to make themselves look, feel, or act superior to anyone is no good to the kingdom of God.

Father sends back to them their own evil, their witchcraft, voodoo, roots, and Santa Rio whatever they use this day back in their own houses. Father it is a new day, and they can never come near my family, Lord get them out of our communities, off our streets and out of our churches in the name of Jesus. Father binds up the airways, making them deaf and dumb to people of God's communication.

Father from the north, southeast and west put hock into their lying tongue. God gives them understanding that what they have done is not a joke but is a disgrace to themselves and to the kingdom of God they small, minded people.

Give unto them all who ask a clean and forgiving heart. Stop them from working iniquity in Your name. Father, I pray that they turn from their wicked ways and come to You. Redeem them Abba Father like I know only can. They have caused too much pain and strife on this earth. I pray that the good citizens of God will never turn a blind eye to these injustices ever again. In Jesus Christ conquering name. So be it.
Amen

Dear reader!

Today, we take our faith to a higher level in Jesus Christ, regarding Your family, health, and finances. Therefore, for every good and pure thing You believe in God for, You can join the Spiritual Agreement page. Write down Your request and sign it!

____

____

Sign____

We the body of believers ask God for supernatural miracles and manifestations according to his word John 14:14, " If ye shall ask anything in my name, I will do it". Thank You, Lord Jesus, in advance for Your care and abundant good blessing in the Mighty name of Jesus!

Amen.

Sincerely, Julian Marie Walker
Author/ Intercessor/ Missionary

20] Prayer for Guidance For Your People

Father in mighty name of Jesus
I pray that You people be set free from false profits. I pray that
Your people have free biases.
I pray that people are free from stereotypes.
I pray that Your people are free from cultural stigma. I pray that
people are free of racism.
I pray that Your people will be free from religious persecution.
I pray that Your people will be free from gender discrimination.
I pray that Your people be free from the lack of financial
opportunity.
I pray that Your people have a free corrupted system.
I pray that Your people be free to unite as one.
I pray that Your people be free from others who are
disrespectful and rude. I pray that people be free from
unethical court practices.
I pray that people be free from unethical school management.
Lord, I pray that people be free from decades of poor laws
and welfare of the states.
I pray that Your people be free from tyrants and
poor leadership. All of the above we give thanks
for in Jesus name.
The prayer of a righteous person has great power to prevail.

Amen

Dear reader!

Today, we take our faith to a higher level in Jesus Christ, regarding Your family, health, and finances. Therefore, for every good and pure thing You believe in God for, You can join the Spiritual Agreement page. Write down Your request and sign it!

____

____

Sign____

We the body of believers ask God for supernatural miracles and manifestations according to his word John 14:14, " If ye shall ask anything in my name, I will do it". Thank You, Lord Jesus, in advance for Your care and abundant good blessing in the Mighty name of Jesus!

Amen.

Sincerely, Julian Marie Walker
Author/ Intercessor/ Missionary

PART 3

**21] Prayer to Acknowledge that there is Power in your
   name.**

Jehovah My God, this hour, and every hour this prayer
will be honored until eternity. All those who used my name
in their mouths to lie or write bad things about me will fall
on their own sword and be put to shame, or in prison. They
will pay and pay greatly for any and all dishonesty with time
and monetary funds.

My name is more than intellectual property; it is an
asset. All those who use my name illegally or my image
improperly, will be punished to the fullest extent of the laws
of the land in the highest court on earth. If anyone removes it
from its rightful place to steal or gain wealth, they also will
be punished and have to answer to the Highest court and my
Father God. It is a solemn promise and seal of Jesus Christ.

Abba Father, my name is for Your glory and honor. My
name is strength, holiness, power, authority, Wisdom,
wealth, compassion, integrity , knowledge. Compassion
ethically, kindness, credit worthiness, justice, and love.

My name is **Julian**. It is blessed and highly favored and it is better than any other name on earth. It will not and never be a compromise for money or anyone or anything. The plan and the purpose of Jesus Christ stands.

This is Jesus Christ my Lord decree and declaration from my birth. In the name of Your Father, son Jesus Christ and Holy Spirit. **The prayer of a righteous man has great power to prevail.**

Amen and Amen

Dear reader!

Today, we take our faith to a higher level in Jesus Christ, regarding Your family, health, and finances. Therefore, for every good and pure thing You believe in God for, You can join the Spiritual Agreement page. Write down Your request and sign it!

____

____

Sign____

We the body of believers ask God for supernatural miracles and manifestations according to his word John 14:14, " If ye shall ask anything in my name, I will do it". Thank You, Lord Jesus, in advance for Your care and abundant good blessing in the Mighty name of Jesus!

Amen.

Sincerely, Julian Marie Walker
Author/ Intercessor/ Missionary

22] Prayer Cry for Justice

Father, I call upon You to awaken the Spirit of my brothers on earth, and all my tribe and my ancestors.
Even the one who has passed. That there will be justice and fairness regarding all that concerning me. This sister cries out to You and asks for help, to see to it that those people who hurt another person again. I give thanks and blessings go up.

The prayer of a righteous man has great power to prevail.

In Jesus name.

Amen

Dear reader!

Today, we take our faith to a higher level in Jesus Christ, regarding Your family, health, and finances. Therefore, for every good and pure thing You believe in God for, You can join the Spiritual Agreement page. Write down Your request and sign it!

____

____

Sign____

We the body of believers ask God for supernatural miracles and manifestations according to his word John 14:14, " If ye shall ask anything in my name, I will do it". Thank You, Lord Jesus, in advance for Your care and abundant good blessing in the Mighty name of Jesus!

Amen.

Sincerely, Julian Marie Walker
Author/ Intercessor/ Missionary

23] The Holy Spirit has Your Way...

Our Father, whose heart is in heaven, gives us this day our daily bread. Father God, I come to You this morning giving thanks and praise to the most high. Father forgive Your people for all their carnality. They are all sick in their minds because they think what they do is right. Father this morning I pray for them, especially those who are caretakers of the sanctuary and guardian of the word of God. So, they should never act like that because they change their clothes, they are perfect but submit themself unto You and stop their evil acts because God is always taking account of the breaking of his commandment which is stealing, lying, and cheating.

Father gives them the wisdom to atone for their own sin. Father I am not judging, but their self-righteous behavior is worse than Lot's wife and Zechariah. Father, we pray for the spirit of the modern-day Ruth on Your women, the spirit of modern-day Moses. I am trusting that You will look over these prayers and You can add the blessing to it or take away anything that is not applicable to You.

Father, I am praying for peace today because wisdom
sees that it is what is needed the most in the country today.
Father, I am calling upon my Psalm 91 God to protect us.
I call You lord to remind You that it is still possible for
Peace to be still, and that no one can break this command.
In the name of the Father, son, and holy Spirit.
The prayer of a righteous man has great power to prevail.
Resounding Amen.

Dear reader!

Today, we take our faith to a higher level in Jesus Christ, regarding Your family, health, and finances. Therefore, for every good and pure thing You believe in God for, You can join the Spiritual Agreement page. Write down Your request and sign it!

____

____

Sign____

We the body of believers ask God for supernatural miracles and manifestations according to his word John 14:14, " If ye shall ask anything in my name, I will do it". Thank You, Lord Jesus, in advance for Your care and abundant good blessing in the Mighty name of Jesus!

Amen.

Sincerely, Julian Marie Walker

Author/ Intercessor/ Missionary

24] Prayer For Divine Healing

Heavenly Father, Thank You for a new day. Father, You said that all things work together for those who love the Lord. I come in Your presence giving thanks in advance because only You know the plans You have for us. So, today we anticipate and hope we put all our trust in You knowing that all things concerning us will be more than good. Father, I know that You are Jehovah Rapha the great physician. Thus, You Lord Jesus declare that with Your stripes we are healed.

Therefore, We pray this day for divine healing to those who believe, will be healed in their bodies, hearts, and mine. I wholeheartedly believe that it is not impossible for Jesus to accomplish this supernatural miracle.
Accordingly, Jesus did it and can still do it again, **Mark 2: 9 - 12 makes us confident.**

9 Which is easier: to say to this paralyzed man, 'Your sins are forgiven,' or to say, 'Get up, take Your mat and walk'? 10 But I want You to know that the Son of Man has authority on earth to forgive sins." So, he said to the man, 11 "I tell You, get up, take Your mat and go home." 12 He got up, took his mat and walked out in full view of them all. This amazed everyone and they praised God, saying, "We have never seen anything like this!" great so, I give You Lord Jesus all the honor and all the praise now in Jesus' mighty name we pray.

Amen.

Dear reader!

Today, we take our faith to a higher level in Jesus Christ, regarding Your family, health, and finances. Therefore, for every good and pure thing You believe in God for, You can join the Spiritual Agreement page. Write down Your request and sign it!

____

____

Sign____

We the body of believers ask God for supernatural miracles and manifestations according to his word John 14:14, " If ye shall ask anything in my name, I will do it". Thank You, Lord Jesus, in advance for Your care and abundant good blessing in the Mighty name of Jesus!

Amen.

Sincerely, Julian Marie Walker
Author/ Intercessor/ Missionary

25] Prayer… God is Our refuge and Strength.

      Heavenly Father, I thank You for being the great I am my refuge and Creator who declares **Peace to be still**. I thank You for being my covering and the power of my strength. According to Psalm 46:1 "God is our refuge and strength, a very present help in trouble." Father with You I have no lack in this world because are with me. Abba Father it's You who strengthen me daily and supply all my needs according to Your riches in heaven.

      I thank You for Your gifts. First and foremost, life and the wisdom to serve You wholeheartedly. A beautiful soul that loves, a heart that truly forgives. Wisdom and first-hand knowledge that You are the power of my strength in all things. The gifts of grace, peace, honesty, kindness, integrity, caring and compassion. Thanks for supernatural and divine favors beyond all human understanding.

Lord Jesus thank You for keeping me through it all. Thank You for closing the wrong doors and opening the right one for me. Thank You for going ahead of me making all the crooked paths straight. Thanks for carrying me when I couldn't walk. Thank You for being my eyes when I could see the dishonesty of friends. Thank You for being my ears, You know I could handle the gossip and lies. My God, I thank You!

Thank You for giving me a new birthday gift every morning when I open my eyes. Thank You for removing all that is corrupt and unclean away from me so that I can fulfill Your purpose. I truly and appreciate the promise, because I am totally aware that this is something no other human in this world can give to me. I thank You for the big dreams that only You, my big and great God, and Lord and Saver, can accomplish through me.
In Jesus Christ name I pray. Amen

Dear reader!

Today, we take our faith to a higher level in Jesus Christ, regarding Your family, health, and finances. Therefore, for every good and pure thing You believe in God for, You can join the Spiritual Agreement page. Write down Your request and sign it!

____

____

Sign____

We the body of believers ask God for supernatural miracles and manifestations according to his word John 14:14, " If ye shall ask anything in my name, I will do it". Thank You, Lord Jesus, in advance for Your care and abundant good blessing in the Mighty name of Jesus!

Amen.

Sincerely, Julian Marie Walker
Author/ Intercessor/ Missionary

26] **Prayer My God of Peace goes beyond anything we can imagine.**

Heavenly Father, we give things for this day, You said to give thanks for all things, great and small and not to worry for anything, just let our request be known through prayers and thanksgiving and You Father is the God of peace. Philippians 4: 6 "Never worry about anything. But in every situation let God know what You need in prayers and requests while giving thanks. **7** Then God's **peace, which goes beyond anything we can imagine, will guard Your thoughts and emotions through Christ Jesus."** So, Abba Father we agree to Your commandment and keep our hope in Your word.
We trust in Your assurance and promise in
Jesus' name. Amen

Dear reader!

Today, we take our faith to a higher level in Jesus Christ, regarding Your family, health, and finances. Therefore, for every good and pure thing You believe in God for, You can join the Spiritual Agreement page. Write down Your request and sign it!

____

____

Sign____

We the body of believers ask God for supernatural miracles and manifestations according to his word John 14:14, " If ye shall ask anything in my name, I will do it". Thank You, Lord Jesus, in advance for Your care and abundant good blessing in the Mighty name of Jesus!

Amen.

Sincerely, Julian Marie Walker
Author/ Intercessor/ Missionary

27] Praying for God People in their time of need

Holy Spirit of God, Thank You for a new day. We give honor and praise to God Almighty, our Savior Lord Jesus Christ. Father because there is none like You. This morning, we give thanks for Your presence of peace and divine harmony. Father, we are aware that there is a strife among some of Your people and so we pray for them in their time of need. Father Your word states in Matthew 5:44, **"But I say to You, love Your enemies, bless those who curse You, do good to those who hate You, and pray for those who spitefully use You and persecute You."**

Lord give them the wisdom to know that You are Lord God Almighty, and You are in charge of all things including the pain in their hearts and emotion. Forgive them first and heal them as You did for so many others. Father it's imperative to forgive them because these hurting people turn around and hurt innocent people. Father God leads Your people not into temptation but delivers them from all evil. Matthew 5:45, **that You may be sons of Your Father in heaven; for He makes his sun rise on the evil and on the good and sends rain on the just and on the unjust."**

May they never again go down the wrong path of life anymore. Father thy is the kingdom and power and glory is Yours. Father, I thank You in advance for divine protection and hope that there is nothing that is impossible for You to do. Father gives all leaders wisdom and strength to do what is right and justified for all Your people. In Jesus name. Amen

Dear reader!

Today, we take our faith to a higher level in Jesus Christ, regarding Your family, health, and finances. Therefore, for every good and pure thing You believe in God for, You can join the Spiritual Agreement page. Write down Your request and sign it!

____

____

Sign____

We the body of believers ask God for supernatural miracles and manifestations according to his word John 14:14, " If ye shall ask anything in my name, I will do it". Thank You, Lord Jesus, in advance for Your care and abundant good blessing in the Mighty name of Jesus!

Amen.

Sincerely, Julian Marie Walker
Author/ Intercessor/ Missionary

28] Friday Faith, we Pray

Father God on this faith Friday we pray for the righteous of
Jesus beloved Christ to take over. There can be any more
hemorrhaging of our blessing. Father, we call on You
Almighty Jehovah God to bind up and lock up all that causes
these problems now and forevermore. Father whether it be a
thing, place, person, or persons.

Lord God, we cry out to You and ask You to intervene now
Lord because enough is enough. Father, it could be the baby
on the breast if they stand against us. Lord, You know the truth
that if they were of us, they would have continued with up, but
Lord they tarry and played games of dishonesty, because the
mind and heart were full of jealousy, deceitful bile lies, stealing,
greed and envy.

Father God my faith believes that there is nothing
You can't do twenty times, twenty and more to those who
partake of sin against Your people earth.   Lord, may
they see the reflection of themselves, that if they plant
good seeds, they will have good harvest, and if they plan
bad seeds intentionally may their own cup runneth over in
their lives. In Jesus' Powerful and mighty name. The son
and the Holy Spirit.
I pray So be it.

Dear reader!

Today, we take our faith to a higher level in Jesus Christ, regarding Your family, health, and finances. Therefore, for every good and pure thing You believe in God for, You can join the Spiritual Agreement page. Write down Your request and sign it!

____

____

Sign____

We the body of believers ask God for supernatural miracles and manifestations according to his word John 14:14, " If ye shall ask anything in my name, I will do it". Thank You, Lord Jesus, in advance for Your care and abundant good blessing in the Mighty name of Jesus!

Amen.

Sincerely, Julian Marie Walker
Author/ Intercessor/ Missionary

29] Morning Prayer The Lord will bless You and keep You

Heavenly Father, We give thanks first and for Your bountiful blessing in Jesus mighty name. Lord, You are good. Father, You are great. Therefore, all honors, praise, glory belong to You. Thank You for keeping and protecting us through the night to see the morning light. We are grateful that You Father God has kept us through the night and kept Your word for all generations.

Jehovah My God, You declare and decree to Moses the Priestly Blessing in Numbers 6:24-26. That The Lord blesses You and keeps You. The Lord makes his face shine on You and be gracious to You. The Lord turns his face toward You and gives You peace. Lord Jesus, we are grateful on this Sabbath morning. Father God because only You can do it like no one else. In everything Lord I give thanks and praise; Jehovah God You are our Rock. Amen and Amen

Dear reader!

Today, we take our faith to a higher level in Jesus Christ, regarding Your family, health, and finances. Therefore, for every good and pure thing You believe in God for, You can join the Spiritual Agreement page. Write down Your request and sign it!

____

____

Sign____

We the body of believers ask God for supernatural miracles and manifestations according to his word John 14:14, " If ye shall ask anything in my name, I will do it". Thank You, Lord Jesus, in advance for Your care and abundant good blessing in the Mighty name of Jesus!

Amen.

Sincerely, Julian Marie Walker
Author/ Intercessor/ Missionary

30] Evening Prayer: God's Plans

Oh Lord, I thank You because Your plans are so awesome. The bible states, accordingly, **Jeremiah 29:11 - For I know the thoughts that I think toward You, saith the LORD, thoughts of peace, and not of evil, to give You an expected end.** Lord Jesus, You are gracious in You all the way towards us.

We give You mighty praise for Your faithfulness, and blessed promises. It's You Lord that declares that You will bless us in the field, and You bless us in the City. You will bless us when we go out and You will bless us when we are coming and father, we hold on to every word because it is a fact. Thank You, Lord, for having the best intention and plans for us. In the name of the Father his son Jesus Christ and the Holy Spirit.

Amen

Dear reader!

Today, we take our faith to a higher level in Jesus Christ, regarding Your family, health, and finances. Therefore, for every good and pure thing You believe in God for, You can join the Spiritual Agreement page. Write down Your request and sign it!

____

____

Sign____

We the body of believers ask God for supernatural miracles and manifestations according to his word John 14:14, " If ye shall ask anything in my name, I will do it". Thank You, Lord Jesus, in advance for Your care and abundant good blessing in the Mighty name of Jesus!

Amen.

Sincerely, Julian Marie Walker
Author/ Intercessor/ Missionary

PART 4

31] Late Night Prayer for Peace - 11:59pm

Lord Jesus, there aren't enough words in the English dictionary for me to use to talk with You tonight. So, I will use groaning. Thus, the Spirit of living God freshly fell on me continues. Father help Your people and comfort them. Father, Your people look like they are dismayed and perplexed in these trying times. Father God gives them peace that passeth all understanding. Father this is Your promise in **2 Thessalonians 3:16, Now the Lord of peace himself gives You peace always by all means. The Lord be with You all.**

I pray this much for all God's people. Give strength to those who need strength. Those who need to be still, let the Holy Spirit take over so that they can be still. Lord, the right action, and behavior is required now.
Subsequently, More peacefully and respectfully than ever before Lord. WE the people canceled the assignment of the devil over families, City, States and Country.
I decree this for all mankind in the name of Father his son Jesus Christ and Holy Spirit.

Amen

Dear reader!

Today, we take our faith to a higher level in Jesus Christ, regarding Your family, health, and finances. Therefore, for every good and pure thing You believe in God for, You can join the Spiritual Agreement page. Write down Your request and sign it!

____

____

Sign____

We the body of believers ask God for supernatural miracles and manifestations according to his word John 14:14, " If ye shall ask anything in my name, I will do it". Thank You, Lord Jesus, in advance for Your care and abundant good blessing in the Mighty name of Jesus!

Amen.

Sincerely, Julian Marie Walker
Author/ Intercessor/ Missionary

32] Jesus asked his Father to forgive mankind

Father Forgive them for they know not what they have done. So, Father today we pray that Your people will come into full knowledge and use wisdom as a teacher. By correcting how they treat each other. Father teaches them that it's a careless presumption to judge any man or woman by their clothes. The truth is the greatest will walk among You and will not know the presence of the Lord.

We must first address the Spirit who willingly gives grace for men or women. Accordingly, I remind You all of this golden story of the **Why? And the What? In Luke 23: 22 For the third time he spoke to them: "Why? What crime has this man committed? I have found in him no grounds for the death penalty. Therefore, I will have him punished and then release him.",** Father Your nation of people is waiting for Your impartation.

Heavenly father may Your people stop assuming and judging each other like they did You. May they experience grace and mercy According, As proven in **Luke 23:34 Jesus said, "Father, forgive them, for they do not know what they are doing."**

And they divided up his clothes by casting lots. May the one wise one have the courage to stand up and say what is not right May they also do what is right and not just to please one man or crowd. In the name of the Father his son Jesus Christ and the Holy Spirit.

Amen

Dear reader!

Today, we take our faith to a higher level in Jesus Christ, regarding Your family, health, and finances. Therefore, for every good and pure thing You believe in God for, You can join the Spiritual Agreement page. Write down Your request and sign it!

____

____

Sign____

We the body of believers ask God for supernatural miracles and manifestations according to his word John 14:14, " If ye shall ask anything in my name, I will do it". Thank You, Lord Jesus, in advance for Your care and abundant good blessing in the Mighty name of Jesus!

Amen.

Sincerely, Julian Marie Walker
Author/ Intercessor/ Missionary

33] Prayer of Truth and Holy Spirit Discernment

Heavenly Father whose heart is in heaven, here I come with the divine Spirit of truth, and of the Holy Ghost which led me. Lord Jesus, may I decrease, and You Father God increase. Lord, I give thanks for revelation. Father God Your word declares that **"the Advocate comes, whom I will send to You from the Father-the Spirit of true When they who proceeds from the Father--He will testify about Me." John 15:26**

Here I go, not putting a name on this gift but acknowledging its powers, love, passion, and its divine presence in the atmosphere. Lord its love, grace, mercy, hope, kindness, and it reveal and seeth all truth. It allows the righteous God to give way to truth, and it gives light to all who are in darkness. The Lord is fair and justified , he embraces all those who believe in the Spirit of God.

Therefore, accordingly to 1 Corinthians 2:4-5 **"My message and my preaching were not with wise and persuasive words, but with a demonstration of the Spirit's power, 5 so that Your faith might not rest on human wisdom, but on God's power."** Father, I pray may our people gain wisdom to heighten their Spirit discernment, for this is good for the father.

In Jesus name, Amen

Dear reader!

Today, we take our faith to a higher level in Jesus Christ, regarding Your family, health, and finances. Therefore, for every good and pure thing You believe in God for, You can join the Spiritual Agreement page. Write down Your request and sign it!

____

____

Sign____

We the body of believers ask God for supernatural miracles and manifestations according to his word John 14:14, " If ye shall ask anything in my name, I will do it". Thank You, Lord Jesus, in advance for Your care and abundant good blessing in the Mighty name of Jesus!

Amen.

Sincerely, Julian Marie Walker
Author/ Intercessor/ Missionary

34] **Armor of Faith**

Heavenly Father we pray for Your strength this way as we permanently put on faith as the whole armor of Our God to stand against anything that might come along. Father, we are aware that we don't wrestle against flesh and blood. Today the Lord binds all principalities and rulers of the darkness.

Father, we are strong in Your powers and cannot be defeated by any spiritual wickedness in high or low places in the world. The devil wiles and evil has no power over any part of our life, our family, our City, Our State or Country in Jesus matchless. We walk on and over its head. We stand for God and are anointed by the Holy Spirit to win and have the Victory.

We have the beauty of righteousness; our breast plate and loins are girting with truth. Our feet are anointed for God's peace with the gospel through God. We put on the helmet of Salvation and the sword of the Spirit of living God. May I remind You that we take the Shield of faith and will defeat the wicked. Accordingly, **Ephesians 6:11 "Above all, taking the shield of faith, wherewith ye shall be able to quench all the fiery darts of the wicked.**

Therefore, also as stated in **Ephesians 6 18 "Praying always with all prayer and supplication in the Spirit and watching thereunto with all perseverance and supplication for all saints; Ephesians 6:19 And for me, that utterance may be given unto me, that I may open my mouth boldly, to make known the mystery of the gospel.**

In Jesus Christ the father of grace and Lord be with all who love our Lord Jesus Christ in sincerity.

Amen

Dear reader!

Today, we take our faith to a higher level in Jesus Christ, regarding Your family, health, and finances. Therefore, for every good and pure thing You believe in God for, You can join the Spiritual Agreement page. Write down Your request and sign it!

____

____

Sign____

We the body of believers ask God for supernatural miracles and manifestations according to his word John 14:14, " If ye shall ask anything in my name, I will do it". Thank You, Lord Jesus, in advance for Your care and abundant good blessing in the Mighty name of Jesus!

Amen.

Sincerely, Julian Marie Walker
Author/ Intercessor/ Mission

35] Prayer for a Discerning Spirit

Father God, we give thanks for this day. Lord Jesus, I know You will have victory in all things. So, Lord, I lay all the justice in the world at Your feet. Accordingly, Proverbs 17:27 "The one who has knowledge uses words with restraint, and whoever has understanding is even-tempered."

"Even fools are thought wise if they keep silent and discerning if they hold their tongues." Proverbs 17 :28 " Therefore, I personally give You thanks in advance in Jesus' mighty name.

Amen

Dear reader!

Today, we take our faith to a higher level in Jesus Christ, regarding Your family, health, and finances. Therefore, for every good and pure thing You believe in God for, You can join the Spiritual Agreement page. Write down Your request and sign it!

____

____

Sign____

We the body of believers ask God for supernatural miracles and manifestations according to his word John 14:14, " If ye shall ask anything in my name, I will do it". Thank You, Lord Jesus, in advance for Your care and abundant good blessing in the Mighty name of Jesus!

Amen.

Sincerely, Julian Marie Walker
Author/ Intercessor/ Missionary

36] For God so loved the World...

     Abba Father, whose heart is in heaven we Your people come to You this day and we proclaim that You are Jesus Christ our Lord and Savior. Father first and Foremost as always, we give thanks and praise in Your name because we Your children know that there is great power and divine favor in Your name. Now we show up and show out in unity to adore You, Oh Great are You Lord, and mighty is Your name.

     We believe that You died on the cross and rise again after the three days for us. Accordingly, John 3:16 declares **"For God so loved the world, that he gave his only begotten Son, that whosoever believeth in him should not perish, but have everlasting life"**. We know it was the greatest act of love for mankind. Lord, You are our redeemer and deliverer of sin. We know that no one before or after can and will achieve and provide this grace for Your people. Father, we praise You forever more.

Father when You say it done; it is so Jehovah my God. Thank You, Lord. Thank You, Lord, for being so wonderful to us.

In Jesus' name we pray. Amen and Amen

Dear reader!

Today, we take our faith to a higher level in Jesus Christ, regarding Your family, health, and finances. Therefore, for every good and pure thing You believe in God for, You can join the Spiritual Agreement page. Write down Your request and sign it!

____

____

Sign____

We the body of believers ask God for supernatural miracles and manifestations according to his word John 14:14, " If ye shall ask anything in my name, I will do it". Thank You, Lord Jesus, in advance for Your care and abundant good blessing in the Mighty name of Jesus!

Amen.

Sincerely, Julian Marie Walker
Author/ Intercessor/ Missionary

37] Ask anything in his name, God will do it.

Abba Father as always, we give thanks because we are human, and we can't do this without You. Lord, I am going to trust that whatever You make allowances for, You would give us the strength to manage it. May the Holy Spirit of God take over and keep us balanced in hearts and minds. Father, we ask for You guidance and protection in all things twenty-four seven, three hundred sixty-five days a year. Father let's make that forevermore because I know You can do more than we could ever ask.

Father this day I pray for all children and their children, children. Father, remember the Covenant and Your promise to keep them safe and they will never beg for bread. They will be healthy, happy, and wise. Father may they all come to know You, that You're the one and true God, who loves them all because You made them.

Father I personal life up my own sons and daughters to You Lord because I believe that You are superior to all and is the living king my Lord and savior Jesus Christ. Father guards and protects them. The Lord cast away anything that would cause them hurt and harm. Father My mom use to say, "A blood that I used to carry them in this world, a no water" So Father today

I put the devil to shame and let him know it is blood I use to carry my kids here in this world and not water, so get thee behind me Satan and run, and run to the bottomless pit of hell never to return. You Satan is now dead and is dust to all mankind. Father gives me strength now to decree and declare in the name of Jesus I have victory. John 14:14 Promised me **"If You]ask anything in My name, I will do it"**. Hallelujah, my God is good. My God is faithful in every area of my life because that is the way God plans it. Fall back all ever evil spirits just know this is the end of You Hallelujah. Thank You, God, Thank You God for doing it I feel a shift in the atmosphere, Hallelujah my King is here.

Thank You, Jesus. In the name of Jesus, Lord take over Jehovah my God got this all.

Amen and Amen
Missionary Julian Marie Walker

Dear reader!

Today, we take our faith to a higher level in Jesus Christ, regarding Your family, health, and finances. Therefore, for every good and pure thing You believe in God for, You can join the Spiritual Agreement page. Write down Your request and sign it!

____

____

Sign____

We the body of believers ask God for supernatural miracles and manifestations according to his word John 14:14, " If ye shall ask anything in my name, I will do it". Thank You, Lord Jesus, in advance for Your care and abundant good blessing in the Mighty name of Jesus!

Amen.

Sincerely, Julian Marie Walker
Author/ Intercessor/ Missionary

38] Prayer God Promise to us.

Abba Father, Whose heart is in heaven we give thanks for this day. Father God, You said that our tongue has great power to do good or evil and so Father today we give thanks and praise and always speak of Your power to do greatness. Accordingly, **"For he that will love life, and see good days, let him refrain his tongue from evil, and his lips that they speak no guile, 1 Peter 3:10** Father God may these words heal and comfort all those that read this prayer for You Jehovah can do all things through the powers of the Holy Spirit.

The good book clearly states that there's a time for every purpose under the heavens. Therefore, whatever the season is for You today by the Almighty God gives You the strength and the powers to prevail. The Lord Jesus will never leave You in Your time of need. God promises is faithful and true, He Father God states that we should, Fear not, for I *am* with You; Be not dismayed, for I *am* Your God. I will strengthen You, Yes, I will help You, I will uphold You with My righteous right hand.'

Glory to God, we give him the highest praise of hallelujah and Amen. Whatever Your greatest needs are, speak to him, God can help You now in the name of Jesus. So, with divine prayers in alignment with the Father's words he will grant favors for all those who believe in his word and power. May the Lord Grant blessing to this prayer in the name of Jesus Christ.

Amen Julian

39] Speak in tongues great, Lord.

Holy Spirit…

Dear reader!

Today, we take our faith to a higher level in Jesus Christ, regarding Your family, health, and finances. Therefore, for every good and pure thing You believe in God for, You can join the Spiritual Agreement page. Write down Your request and sign it!

____

____

Sign____

We the body of believers ask God for supernatural miracles and manifestations according to his word John 14:14, " If ye shall ask anything in my name, I will do it". Thank You, Lord Jesus, in advance for Your care and abundant good blessing in the Mighty name of Jesus!

Amen.

Sincerely, Julian Marie Walker
Author/ Intercessor/ Missionary

40] Prayer, WE abide in the True Vine

Heavenly Father, we thank You this day for abiding in me. Thanks for courage and comprehension in bearing good fruits. We know who You are, and we give You all praise. The Father God. John 15:5 states **"I am the vine; You *are* the branches. He who abides in Me, and I in him, bears much fruit; for without Me You can do nothing.** Father, we know that the Holy Spirit makes allowance for us all in all circumstances.

The greatest strength and courage I know Lord is to come to You as we are and knowing that You Lord Jesus will greet and love us with open arms. Father Your people are reaching out to You this day for love, peace, guidance, harmony, wisdom, courage, comfort, and compassion. Father, we know You are the head of our lives. The key to our love and happiness. The root to our passion and joy. The king of our faith, hope and trust. **John 15: 11 also states "These things I have spoken to You, that My joy may remain in You, and *that* Your joy may be full. 12 This is My commandment, that You love one another as I have loved You.**

Father this sabbath we honor You in all that we do and say. Father, we trust You, and we know that when You open doors no mediocre man or woman can't close. Father, we thank You for Your awesome power to sustain us in everything we do and say. Great are You, Lord. We declare that we are the heir of the true vine, roots and branches that never wither because You Jesus Christ said so. Mighty is Your word and name.

In Jesus Christ name we pray, Amen

Dear reader!

Today, we take our faith to a higher level in Jesus Christ, regarding Your family, health, and finances. Therefore, for every good and pure thing You believe in God for, You can join the Spiritual Agreement page. Write down Your request and sign it!

____

____

Sign____

We the body of believers ask God for supernatural miracles and manifestations according to his word John 14:14, " If ye shall ask anything in my name, I will do it". Thank You, Lord Jesus, in advance for Your care and abundant good blessing in the Mighty name of Jesus!

Amen.

Sincerely, Julian Marie Walker
Author/ Intercessor/ Missionary

PAGE 5

41] Prayer God's faithfulness and truth

Heavenly Father, we give thanks this day because the Lord is good, he is faithful and truth, his mercy endureth for all generations. **"O Lord, thou art my God; I will exalt thee, I will praise thy name; for thou hast done wonderful things; thy counsels of old are faithfulness and truth".**
Isaiah 25:1. Therefore beloved ,I was glad when they said unto me let go and worship in the house of the Lord. Accordingly, we prayed, and You answered with an abundance of blessing for a lifetime. The bible declares when two more are gathered together in Your name You Father God will be there, so Abba father there is here today.

Holy Spirit of living God, we greet You in secret of the highest place this morning. In full knowledge that You Lord Jesus have us in Your tender care, and no harm from anyone can come near us. Lord Jesus we are confident that You are the supreme ruler over all mankind, and You are faithful in ministering truth, providing, and protecting us. Father, You give peace and happiness like no other so, let the record show that we are blessed, and we are grateful forevermore.

Oh father, we give You all the honor, praise, and glory. We magnified Your great and righteous name Jehovah our banner. We pray that this day everything and everyone in heaven and earth will come in alignment for the edification of Your people. Thank You, Lord, in advance for all You are doing right now. The Spirit of the living God will have his way. I pray so be it.

Amen

Dear reader!

Today, we take our faith to a higher level in Jesus Christ, regarding Your family, health, and finances. Therefore, for every good and pure thing You believe in God for, You can join the Spiritual Agreement page. Write down Your request and sign it!

____

____

Sign____

We the body of believers ask God for supernatural miracles and manifestations according to his word John 14:14, " If ye shall ask anything in my name, I will do it". Thank You, Lord Jesus, in advance for Your care and abundant good blessing in the Mighty name of Jesus!

Amen.

Sincerely, Julian Marie Walker
Author/ Intercessor/ Missionary

42] Prayer Big Thanks Father God

Heavenly Father God, we thank You for this beautiful and bright day. We thank You for taking care of our families and loved ones. The Bible teaches us that everything that has breath Praise ye the Lord. Accordingly, **Psalm 150:6 " Let everything that hath breath praise the Lord. Praise ye the Lord".** Therefore, Father God I will, I shall and promised to forever praise You as my personal Lord and Savior. Father God, maybe I am the first to say this to You, but wholeheartedly I give BIG thanks and Praise to You because You deserve it.

Thank You for never putting my hope and trust in You to shame. Thank You for always being here and there for me. Holy Spirit of God thank You for bestowing the blessing of faith, hope, grace, peace, health, wisdom, strength, wealth, happiness, love, joy, beauty, and assurance. Father God with You charge I lack nothing. I believe and know that You are a wonderful working God, and no man has the capability to undo my blessing or permanently steal what You God has provided for me. God will intervene in a mighty, mighty way because He loves me, this I know.

Father God in Your promise You said that heaven and earth would come to pass if Your word is void. Accordingly, **Heaven and earth will pass away, but My words will never pass away,"** Matthew 24:25 Father I don't worry because I believe You will and shall take care of all the soul, and mind playing demons and give them notice that yesterday was their last day of stealing, lies and trouble making in heaven and on earth.

 I thank You Lord if they miss the memo let them see it for themselves today and fall off. Lord, I thank You for a wonderful life and I receive Your love and blessing in Jesus' mighty name.

Amen

Dear reader!

Today, we take our faith to a higher level in Jesus Christ, regarding Your family, health, and finances. Therefore, for every good and pure thing You believe in God for, You can join the Spiritual Agreement page. Write down Your request and sign it!

____

____

Sign____

We the body of believers ask God for supernatural miracles and manifestations according to his word John 14:14, " If ye shall ask anything in my name, I will do it". Thank You, Lord Jesus, in advance for Your care and abundant good blessing in the Mighty name of Jesus!

Amen.

Sincerely, Julian Marie Walker
Author/ Intercessor/ Missionary

43] Evening Prayer

Heavenly Father, We thank You for this precious day. Thank You for all things You have done for us all, even the big and small surprises . I am most grateful for all Your yes, that showed us that You had everything in Your control every moment. Blessing is truly a gift from God. *Won't he do, it is still my praise.*

Amen

Dear reader!

Today, we take our faith to a higher level in Jesus Christ, regarding Your family, health, and finances. Therefore, for every good and pure thing You believe in God for, You can join the Spiritual Agreement page. Write down Your request and sign it!

____

____

Sign____

We the body of believers ask God for supernatural miracles and manifestations according to his word John 14:14, " If ye shall ask anything in my name, I will do it". Thank You, Lord Jesus, in advance for Your care and abundant good blessing in the Mighty name of Jesus!

Amen.

Sincerely, Julian Marie Walker
Author/ Intercessor/ Missionary

44] Prayer The Spirit Of Lord Rest On Us

 Heavenly Father I lift my hands to You in awesome wonder and praise. We, Your people, give thanks for Your guidance, provision, and protection. Father, we acknowledge that You Lord are great and are the worthy lion and the lamb. Accordingly, You Lord pour out the Holy Spirit on Your chosen people, **"And the spirit of the Lord shall rest upon him, the spirit of wisdom and understanding, the spirit of counsel and might, the spirit of knowledge and of the fear of the Lord", Isaiah 11:2**

Father, we give thanks for the miracles You do today. Thank You for never forgetting Your people's prayers. The Lord is my shepherd; I shall not want. Father we pour out our praise through the holy spirit, accordingly, **Acts 2:4 All of them were filled with the Holy Spirit and began to speak in other tongues as the Spirit enabled them.** We received by faith and in the name Jesus Christ. We pray always giving honor and thanksgiving to You oh Lord, our God, and the Holy Spirit.

Amen and Amen

Dear reader!

Today, we take our faith to a higher level in Jesus Christ, regarding Your family, health, and finances. Therefore, for every good and pure thing You believe in God for, You can join the Spiritual Agreement page. Write down Your request and sign it!

____

____

Sign____

We the body of believers ask God for supernatural miracles and manifestations according to his word John 14:14, " If ye shall ask anything in my name, I will do it". Thank You, Lord Jesus, in advance for Your care and abundant good blessing in the Mighty name of Jesus!

Amen.

Sincerely, Julian Marie Walker
Author/ Intercessor/ Missionary

45] Blessed Day

Heavenly Father, I thank You for this blessed day. I come to You as I am, withholding nothing. Thank You for ministering to me on this blessed day. I am saved because You died for me. I am strong because You give me strength. I love You because You love me first and it's so. I am happy because You give me joy. I am healthy because You are a doctor. Father, thank You for protecting me. I have peace because You are my father God.

Abba Father, please protect my children and grandchildren may they never have any lack or need in Jesus' name. According to **I come offering Praise be to the God and Father of our Lord Jesus Christ, who has blessed us in the heavenly realms with every spiritual blessing in Christ. 4 For he chose us in him before the creation of the world to be holy and blameless in his sight. Ephesians 1:3-4**

LORD, You promised that our people's hands and hearts will always favor and always provide good things for us. Thank You for being our healer, provider, and protector. Thank You for forgiving us of all faults and any transgression. Father if we have sin or hurt anyone, we ask for pardon in the name of the Father God, his Son Jesus Christ, and the Holy Spirit. Father, as You put a seal on this prayer, may You add a blessing onto, in Jesus Christ Holy and Miraculous name.

Selah and Amen

Dear reader!

Today, we take our faith to a higher level in Jesus Christ, regarding Your family, health, and finances. Therefore, for every good and pure thing You believe in God for, You can join the Spiritual Agreement page. Write down Your request and sign it!

____

____

Sign____

We the body of believers ask God for supernatural miracles and manifestations according to his word John 14:14, " If ye shall ask anything in my name, I will do it". Thank You, Lord Jesus, in advance for Your care and abundant good blessing in the Mighty name of Jesus!

Amen.

Sincerely, Julian Marie Walker
Author/ Intercessor/ Missionary

46] Prayer for God to Change People's Wicked Ways

      Father God, I humble myself only to You with a clean heart that You are Jesus Christ the son of God and fully knowing You are one and only true God. I give thanks to You always because You are living Jesus Christ our Lord. Today I pray for fairness and justice for all people. Nevertheless, for those practicing evil Communication. Father put them to shame.

      My God, may You pay them back with their own medicine and cut them off from other people's money and blessings. **1st Corinthians 15:3 "Be not deceived: evil communications corrupt good manners.** They seem to forget this verse when they indulge in witchcraft from their altars. **Jeremiah 5: 4" Therefore I said, Surely these *are* poor; they are foolish: for they know not the way of the LORD, *nor* the judgment of their God".**

Father Your words according to the Bible states **"For among my people are found wicked *men*: they lay wait, as he that setteth snares; they set a trap, they catch men."Jer.5:26.** Thus, I declare in the name of the Father and his son Jesus Christ and the Holy Spirit that they will fall in their pit and web of lies and deceit because God said in **Jeremiah 5:29 'Shall I not punish *them* for these *things*?' declares the LORD, 'Or shall I not avenge Myself, On a nation such as this?'**

Father there must be a stop now and Justice must prevail.

O God shut down all their lines of communication, their operations and business. Father stops their wicked action against God righteous people. Take away their licenses to partake and operate in the marketplaces. Lord, You said and acknowledge, **2nd Chronicles 7:14 "If my people, which are called by my name, shall humble themselves, and pray, and seek my face, and turn from their wicked ways; then will I hear from heaven, and will forgive their sin, and will heal their land.** I thank You in advance In Jesus name.

Amen

Dear reader!

Today, we take our faith to a higher level in Jesus Christ, regarding Your family, health, and finances. Therefore, for every good and pure thing You believe in God for, You can join the Spiritual Agreement page. Write down Your request and sign it!

____

____

Sign____

We the body of believers ask God for supernatural miracles and manifestations according to his word John 14:14, " If ye shall ask anything in my name, I will do it". Thank You, Lord Jesus, in advance for Your care and abundant good blessing in the Mighty name of Jesus!

Amen.

Sincerely, Julian Marie Walker
Author/ Intercessor/ Missionary

47] Prayer God Turned It Around

Father, I thank You because late in the night God, You
show me great favor and turn it around. What they meant for
evil exalted me and lifted me up to a great place of power,
position and great wealth, and respect. Father, I thank You,
You have used every brick and block they have thrown at me
to break down every wall of opposition that stands in my way.
I am free and I conduct all my affairs with integrity and good
moral ethics according to the plans and purposes of God.
Thank You, Lord, for being a good, and great God, Father, I
thank You. Great are You LORD.

The LORD declares I am Blessed and highly favored
forevermore in Jesus Mighty Name.

Amen and Amen

Dear reader!

Today, we take our faith to a higher level in Jesus Christ, regarding Your family, health, and finances. Therefore, for every good and pure thing You believe in God for, You can join the Spiritual Agreement page. Write down Your request and sign it!

____

____

Sign____

We the body of believers ask God for supernatural miracles and manifestations according to his word John 14:14, " If ye shall ask anything in my name, I will do it". Thank You, Lord Jesus, in advance for Your care and abundant good blessing in the Mighty name of Jesus!

Amen.

Sincerely, Julian Marie Walker
Author/ Intercessor/ Missionary

48] **Prayer Jesus declared, "I am the bread of life"**

Heavenly Father, We give heavenly thanks unto You because You are still a miracle worker and wonder working God. Thank You for upholding the promised covenant You made with my family. I give You all the Glory and the honor this day for being my way maker and wondering God. Father, You said it and declared if we follow You accordingly, we would never be hungry or thirst for nothing.

LORD You words states in **John 6: 35 Then Jesus declared, "I am the bread of life. Whoever comes to me will never go hungry, and whoever believes in me will never be thirsty.** Therefore, my God fed over five thousand people with two fish and five loaves of bread and had enough left over. I know You God can do all things. This day I put all my concerns and hope in Your hands. I wait for the Miracles You will do again and again.

Thank You, LORD, it's You who said Greater is HE that is in me than of this World. I received by Faith in Jesus ' mighty name accordingly, **John 4:4 "Ye are of God, little children, and have overcome them: because greater is he that is in You, than he that is in the world."** May the Lord add all blessings to my prayers in Jesus Christ Holy name I pray.

Amen

Dear reader!

Today, we take our faith to a higher level in Jesus Christ, regarding Your family, health, and finances. Therefore, for every good and pure thing You believe in God for, You can join the Spiritual Agreement page. Write down Your request and sign it!

____

____

Sign____

We the body of believers ask God for supernatural miracles and manifestations according to his word John 14:14, " If ye shall ask anything in my name, I will do it". Thank You, Lord Jesus, in advance for Your care and abundant good blessing in the Mighty name of Jesus!

Amen.

Sincerely, Julian Marie Walker
Author/ Intercessor/ Missionary

49] Prayer Missionary Prayer

LORD JESUS, I thank You for giving me and the Church and US, the grace, empathy of awareness to provide good services to all mankind and those in need emotionally, spiritually, physically, and financially. Thank You for giving us the courage and strength to continue the Lord's work with a kind and caring heart. Father, we ask that through the Holy Spirit, You will guide us to be fair and honest when dealing with all Your people regardless gender, race, religion, creed, or nationality.

Lord give us eyes to see, ears to hear wisdom to operate in decency and order. May we have spiritual gifts to bring souls to You. May we have healing hands of angels to care for Your people. May we have strong feet like Moses to go the distance to ensure a great harvest to edify Your name. May we have more than enough oil in our lamps to shine through the darkness. May we have enough bread and water to feed You people. May we all have divine protection and favor in Jesus' name. May we be good stewards of each other starting at home in our Churches, School Communities, States, Country, and Nation.

May We always be on our best behavior and uphold
the integrity of God and Country. Father Accordingly we
accept Your will as You stated Matthew **18-20** And Jesus came
and said to them, "All authority in heaven and on earth has
been given to me. **19 Go therefore and make disciples of all
nations, baptizing them in the name of the Father and of
the Son and of the Holy Spirit, 20 teaching them to
observe all that I have commanded You. And behold, I am
with You always, to the end of the age."** Matthew 28 18 20.

In Jesus' name we pray thank You, and God's people say,
Amen and Amen.

Missionary Julian Marie Walker

Dear reader!

Today, we take our faith to a higher level in Jesus Christ, regarding Your family, health, and finances. Therefore, for every good and pure thing You believe in God for, You can join the Spiritual Agreement page. Write down Your request and sign it!

____

____

Sign_______________________________________

We the body of believers ask God for supernatural miracles and manifestations according to his word John 14:14, " If ye shall ask anything in my name, I will do it". Thank You, Lord Jesus, in advance for Your care and abundant good blessing in the Mighty name of Jesus!

Amen.

Sincerely, Julian Marie Walker
Author/ Intercessor/ Missionary

50] An Intimate talk and walk with Jesus Christ

Heavenly Father, I thank You for being a merciful and kind Father to me. It would take a thousand lifetimes to thank You and tell the World how good You are to me. Father it still amazes people that no matter what is going on in m y life You adore and cherish me. Father, thank You for being my rock and my harmony and peace. Thank You for always holding my hands.

When the trial of life comes You hide me and sustain me. I live in the goodness of God our Father. I am truly grateful, and I vow to You that You LORD will always be my first love in Jesus' mighty name I pray.

Amen

Missionary Julian Marie Walker

Dear reader!

Today, we take our faith to a higher level in Jesus Christ, regarding Your family, health, and finances. Therefore, for every good and pure thing You believe in God for, You can join the Spiritual Agreement page. Write down Your request and sign it!

____

____

Sign____

We the body of believers ask God for supernatural miracles and manifestations according to his word John 14:14, " If ye shall ask anything in my name, I will do it". Thank You, Lord Jesus, in advance for Your care and abundant good blessing in the Mighty name of Jesus!

Amen.

Sincerely, Julian Marie Walker
Author/ Intercessor/ Missionary

About the Author

Ms. Julian Marie Walker was born in Clarendon, Jamaica, West Indies. She lived in New York for over thirty years and attended Metropolitan College of New York and attended the Metropolitan College of New York where she earned a Bachelor's in Professional Studies. She is also a graduate of Ohio Christian University with a Master's in Business Administration. She has been blessed by God to be a mother of five children, five grandchildren, and one great-grand.

She attends and is a member of Tabernacle of Praise Church International, in McDonough GA, while also worshiping and serving as a greeter at the Griffin Campus. She serves on the TOPCI prayer team as an Intercessory for leadership and the needs of the entire congregation. The team is known as the Church Prayer Warriors. She has also helped to launch and worked as a volunteer for the TJMM Ministry. The church was founded and is still operated by the Bishop-Elect T.J. McBride and his wife, the beautiful and apostolic Pastor Shunnae McBride.

One of her greatest passions and purposes in life is that she is a missionary, serving at Tabernacle of Praise Church International, Global Mission Ministry under the guidance of Minister Christ Scott and Minister Lori Sunshine. The guard was recently changed to our new director Minister Sandra James who has served faithfully for years. Ms. Walker served as a missionary locally and Internationally in Belize, Haiti, and the Dominican Republic. She works in the distribution of food, and fellowship, working in hospitals, and medical clinics, visiting the elders and orphanages, and building schools and churches.

Ms. Walker is a well-cultured, caring Christian, with a Godly heritage and is committed to faith, moral ethics, and integrity with the desire to further the growth of this organization through the advancement and empowerment of all people. Not just in my community and regardless of nationality, but to all people. Subsequently, Thus, I have a servant's heart that believes that the great servant makes the greatest leaders in history. Her volunteering, work experience, contribution, and exceeding the standards define my true character and achievements in putting my mother's greatest gift to me which is the gift of powers of prayers.

Acknowledgments

My thanks to my Bishop, and Pastors for sharing their love for us and humanity. Thanks to TOPCI mission team members past and present who have served and given wholeheartedly to advance humankind in a spirit of love and kindness for the kingdom of God. I salute You all one love. Thanks, Dr. Patricia Bailey for teaching us and showing us love for mankind around the world. Thank You, Dr. Chris Scott I have Connect the Dots. Thanks, Mama Patrick for imparted wisdom and experience of being of missionary. Thanks, Ms. Yasmine, and others for Your sponsoring financial support. Big, big thanks Deacon Cail for always seeing that we all got home safe. Thanks, Mother Maxine thanks for always praying tour bus. much respect for the founders of Life Beyond Water a Church without Walls. Thanks, Min. Sunshine for encouraging me in my journal on my mission trip.

Credit is given to the entire team, Pastor Scott, and Dr. Will, Min. Lori, Min. Sandra, Melissa, Michael, Min. Eric, Deaconess Antoinette, Lawrence, Min. Samantha, Sister Coral, Ms. Collins, Felica, Min. Lynda, Lydia, Lisa, Debra, Min. Kayle, Jules, Ceria, Min. Mama and Papa Patrick, Martha, Troy, Yolanda Hart Amina, and others.

Praise God we go to Nation!

Dedication

In memory of my mother, Victoria Marie Brown-Hyde; my father, Justin Walker; and my brother, Trooper Upton J. Walker, I give thanks.

Thankful for the strength of God, my children, grandchildren, great-grandchildren, and my nieces and nephews.

All missionaries around I pray for continued protection and provision.

www.ingramcontent.com/pod-product-compliance
Lightning Source LLC
Chambersburg PA
CBHW061531050726
47593CB00002B/755